Copyright © Marcus Jackson, 2021

ISBN: 9798454813611

All rights reserved. No part of this book may be reproduced or used in any manner without written permission of the copyright owner except for the use of quotations in a book review. For more information, address: drmarcjack@yahoo.com.

10 Daily Essentials for Assistant Principals

(Tips for Having an Effective, Efficient, Efficacious Day)

By

Marcus Jackson, Ed.D.

Table of Contents

FOREWORD vi

Acknowledgment viii

Introduction 10

The 10 Daily Essentials 13

Essential 1:
Awaken Excited About the Day 13

Essential 2:
Establish an Inspirational Routine for the Morning Commute 21

Essential 3:
Arrive Early and Be Prepared to Be the Principal ... 25

Essential 4:
Greet Every Student and Staff Member 36

Essential 5:
Visit Your Students, Teachers and Conduct Positive Walkthroughs 40

Essential 6:
Morning Meeting with Your Principal 56

Essential 7:
Live in the Organizational Framework: Know all Master Two 60

Essential 8:
Establish an Extinguishing System 67

Essential 9:

Make Your Instructional Presence Felt: Cycle of Academic Excellence **72**

Essential 10:

Keep the Triangle Connected: Parents, Student, School (Administration and Teachers) **102**

- Find a Need Fill the Gap (Be Extraordinary) ... **102**
- Find a Need Fill in the Gap **109**

Bonus:

Most Essential of the Essentials: **112**

Reflect, Revise, Write, and Relax **112**

References **117**

FOREWORD

By: Dr. Chike Akua

I first met Dr. Marcus Jackson almost ten years ago. I quickly became deeply impressed with the style and substance of his leadership as a principal, then as the Director of Curriculum and Instruction where he turned around the fourteen lowest-performing schools in his district. Dr. Jackson is both strategic and intuitive in his approach. He leads with head and heart. He has his finger on the pulse of the leaders, teachers, students, and communities he serves. As a result, he has produced consistent, outstanding results even amid repeated, severe community crises (devastating violence, hurricanes, and COVID-19, just to name a few).

I have often said that leadership is "organizing and mobilizing people and resources to meet needs and solve problems." Organizing means bringing people together. This is something Dr. Jackson does very well. He helps leaders, teachers, and communities come together to help students. Mobilizing means being on the move toward a common purpose. Some people are together, but they're not moving. Some are moving, but they're not together. Dr. Jackson organizes and mobilizes those he serves.

Some leaders have organized and mobilized people but have no resources. Some have resources but only have undeveloped people. Dr. Jackson organizes people and resources very effectively. Finally, he empowers those he serves to meet needs and solve problems--and that's what it's all about. If you're not meeting needs and solving problems, you are not involved in leadership or education.

So, I am pleased to recommend this book to leaders and aspiring leaders from one who demonstrates leadership at the highest level. This book is not just to be read. It is to be studied, highlighted, and implemented over and over. Take each of the essentials that he shares seriously. Then, you too can produce outstanding results.

Many think low-performing schools can't be changed, but Dr. Marcus Jackson has achieved remarkable results leading at every level. For educational leaders who are serious about transforming some of the most challenging schools, Dr. Marcus Jackson's 10 Daily Essentials for Assistant Principals is a must-read!

Acknowledgment

I would like to take a few minutes to acknowledge a few individuals who we critical in beginning my educational leadership journey. First, I would like to acknowledge my former principal Catalina Silbilsky who saw educational leadership potential in me when I was a teacher at Morningside Elementary School. Secondly, I would like to thank Dr. Douglas Hendrix who I watched from afar a listened as he Derrick Thomas and Dr. Keith Colbert would engage in intellectual dialogue in between pickup basketball games. It was during this point I decided to become an assistant principal.

After twenty-six interviews, I was awarded the position of assistant principal at Hawthorne Elementary School. Under the leadership of Dr. Wynton Walker my educational leadership seeds were planted, fertilized, and nurtured. We would meet every Monday morning to discuss plans for the week. During these meetings she would not only welcome my new ideas and innovative initiatives, but she provided me with an example of critical leadership lessons on delegation, effective instructional leadership, organizing teams, coaching, and risk taking. Most importantly, she assigned several duties to me that we're the responsibility of the principal. For example, I was heavily involved with the Title I budget, School Improvement Plan, Parent Involvement Plan, After School Remediation, and meetings with stakeholders. You name it I did it. Many students thought I was the principal.

After receiving a plethora of on-the-job training, I had the opportunity to become principal as six weeks into my first year as an assistant principal, my principal went out for a procedure, and I was the administrator for four weeks. During this time, I leaned heavily on mentors Jocelyn Brown, Dr. Anthony Smith, Dean Lillard and Clarence Jackson. Also, the phenomenal assistant principals I had the luxury of working with Latonya Paige, Dr. Trina Reeves, Stacy Black, Dennis Williamson, and Nelson Render, Dr. Valencia Bryant, and Earnest Sessoms. In conclusion, I would like to thank everyone in Clayton County Public Schools for providing me with a strong educational leadership foundation. It was there the Dr. Jackson that you know of today was born. I am forever grateful.

Introduction

10 Daily Essentials for Assistant Principals:

Tips for an Effective, Efficient, Efficacious Day

Whether you are a new assistant principal, or a decades-plus assistant principal—being an instructional leader in your building is an important, rewarding, yet demanding job. As an assistant principal, you will face frustrating moments—a non-stop inbox with seemingly, impossible deadlines; irate parents; meetings about meetings, all while being expected to overcome day-to-day, herculean obstacles. Undoubtedly, a few of the challenges will be:

1.) Designing and implementing a rigorous, culturally relevant curriculum.
2.) Managing daily, building operations, and logistics.
3.) Overseeing an ever-dwindling budget.
4.) Conducting teacher evaluations.
5.) Dealing with several behavior issues

Having pre-knowledge of all these known factors is beneficial; however, it is imperative for you, as the assistant principal, to plan your day to accommodate the unknown as well. And so, you will create a To Do List, and you will prioritize the items on your To Do List, based on deadlines, resources, needs, etc. You will set calendar reminders, and communicate with your administrative assistant, and your administrative team to ensure that the integral players are apprised of your well-planned day. And just as the poet, Robert Burns, so eloquently stated, *the best-laid plans of mice and men often go awry*...rest assured that your well-planned day, will deviate from your To Do List, and it will disregard your need to accomplish tasks in a timely manner. Whether you are a new assistant principal, or a decades-plus assistant principal, in these moments—you will be frustrated—if you do not plan, and over plan—even for your frustration, you can and will find yourself to at the center of a disastrous day— and it's only 9:30 a.m. How do you overcome the inevitable and ensure that your best-laid plans stay the course throughout the day? As a former principal at the elementary, middle, and high school levels and assistant principal at the elementary level, I was able to garner success—regardless of the obstacles. These pragmatic practices are the solid foundation that you will need to build a better day—every day. I call them *10 Daily Essentials*.

The Significance of the Assistant Principal

The Assistant Principal Position is critical to the success of the school. They serve as a bridge between the teachers, staff, and the principal. They will usually have a better assessment of the school's pulse as many times, and teachers are more comfortable speaking to them about issues on their grade level and concerns that may affect the school's culture. An assistant principals' ability to maintain confidentiality and trust with their teachers and discuss them with the principal is vital to the school's success.

-Dr. Marcus D. Jackson

The 10 Daily Essentials

Essential 1:

Awaken Excited About the Day

Every morning when I awake, I am not only filled with energy, excitement, and enthusiasm about being blessed to see another day, but I am elated to be in a leadership position that allows me to enhance children's lives, and to inspire teachers. All of us have this same opportunity.

Every night, we lay our heads on our pillows, and we go to sleep. We wake up to a new day, with new opportunities to do something amazing. At that moment, we can choose to get out of bed and make the most of our day. We can approach our day by saying, *I am blessed to be able to go to work.* Or we can press the snooze button; roll over—pull the blankets over our heads, while thinking, *I have to go to work!* There is a difference. I choose to say, *I get to go to work to fulfill my mission and my purpose.* Our mindset is our choice. Generally, the way we start our day will influence how we will feel for the rest of the day.

Let's look at five, fast ways we can start our day off on a positive note:

1.) Set your daily alarm clock fifteen minutes early; this allows you time to wake up and begin your day. Additionally, if you are prone to press the infamous snooze button, you will still be on time.

2.) When you wake up in the morning, take a moment to appreciate the new opportunity that you have been given. Take some deep breaths and find something that you are grateful for—your children; your partner; your health; your career. Take time to be thankful for all that you have in your life, rather than focusing on the negative, or the inevitable things that you cannot change. Whatever you lack, will come. What happened yesterday, is in the past. The irate parent that you have to meet with—just wants to be heard. The upcoming IEP meeting with the advocate, and the district's instructional focus walk throughs—none of these things should be your focal point, until you have made a commitment to have a productive day, steeped in positivity. Your thoughts will become your actions, and your actions will speak louder than anything you will say.

3.) Drink water—before doing anything else. Whether you make a cup of green tea, or merely drink the bottle of water on your nightstand—morning hydration is imperative. During the night, it is easy for us to get dehydrated—and coffee can exacerbate this condition. Therefore, begin your day with some type of water; this will support blood circulation, as well as healthy brain, and organ function. These simple, yet mindful acts will lay the foundation for you to have an awesome day.

4.) Start the day off with a healthy breakfast. You will need to foster and sustain your energy throughout the day; however, that electrifying energy will be most important when you arrive to work. Because of this--your breakfast should not be too heavy, but rather, it should be something light, but packed with protein—a fortified green smoothie; a fruit cup; a protein bar, or my favorite—oatmeal. Raisins and brown sugar are optional but recommended.

5.) Set your intentions for a positive, productive day. Visualize a positive outcome for the tasks of the day that have potential for discord, or for confusion. The irate parent—visualize beginning and ending the meeting positively. Visualize every aspect of the meeting going well. See yourself in the IEP meeting—with the advocate. See the positive outcomes that best support the needs of the student. Oh—and the feedback from the district's walkthrough—that too, will be positive—if you first visualize the outcomes. To manifest, and to create this kind of positivity—you must believe it. You must bring it into your mind, into your heart, and into your spirit. You must ensure that your intentions for your day are fixed. You must first conceive it to achieve it. You control the vectors of your day—ensure that you begin every day with a positive outlook.

Most people fail to understand the power of their thoughts. However, one's daily outlook has a tremendous impact on one's future. Here is one of my favorite stories that illustrates this altruistic point.

Perception

Your self-perception is vital to becoming a better version of yourself, every day. How do you view life? Are you an optimist—do you see the proverbial glass as half full? Or are you a pessimist—the glass is always half empty? Either way you see it—you are correct because it is your perception of yourself, others, and situations that validate what you see.

I once heard a story about two men who were patients in the same hospital room. Every day, the man closest to the window shared with his new friend what he saw outside; he described in detail, the people, the clouds, the sounds of nature—everything. He meticulously described what he saw, so his roommate could enjoy the view—even though both of them were confined to hospital beds.

Today, I see a beautiful sunrise, he'd say. *The sky is a mixture of blues, yellows, and flecks of orange. And the kids are already out there playing. The trees are in full bloom—so there are many shades of green.* Each day, the man would go on and on—in full detail. And each day, the bedridden friend looked forward to hearing his roommate's report on the outside world. Truthfully, it was the highlight of their day.

One day, the patient next to the window grew excited. *Oh, you should see it! There's a parade coming by—with a marching band...can you hear it? Everyone looks so cheerful—kids and adults alike are smiling, dancing, and having such a good time.* Sadly, after several weeks, the patient next to the window passed away. The remaining patient asked the nurse if he could move to the bed next to the window, where his friend had laid, and shared a new report, every day. He, too, wanted to see all the great scenes that his roommate had so impressively described.

The nurse obliged her patient. She enlisted the help of a colleague to transfer the patient from one bed to the next. Gingerly, they moved the patient, and he teemed with excitement; he could not wait to see the sights that the window promised to reveal. But once the man was situated, he looked out the window, and much to his surprise—all he saw was a brick wall. About fifteen feet away stood another wing of the hospital. The patient called the nurse back in, and said, *Hey, wait a minute! What's going on? My friend, before he died, described so many beautiful scenes— every day, every week! But I can't see anything but a wall! The nurse smiled and said, Sir, didn't you realize that your friend was blind? Still, he chose to see a beautiful world. And he chose to share those visions with you. What a friend indeed.*

Regardless of the twists and turns your life takes, you can find the good—if you look for it. If you have the right attitude, you can see the beautiful sun shining—even when it is cloudy outside. You can be joyful and continue to improve—even when things do not seem to go as planned. Make a commitment to live every day with enthusiasm and optimism. Wake up each morning and say aloud all the things for which you are grateful; make a list. Keep the list close to you, and each day pursue your dreams. Each day have a new resolve to be better than you were the day before. Understand that your day has purpose, and that every day is your day! Your voice should be the first voice you hear—speak positively over yourself, and over your day. Every day, tell yourself, *I am awesome. I am amazing, and I am prepared for this phenomenal day.*

The Significance of the Assistant Principal

"You'll never change your life until you change something you do daily. The secret of your success is found in your daily routine."

~ John C. Maxwell

Essential 2:

Establish an Inspirational Routine for the Morning Commute

The average leader has a commute time of 25-45 minutes. This time can be dedicated to ensuring that your workday goes well. Use these tips to be productive during your commute:

- Tune in to a podcast, or listen to inspirational audio books, or inspirational music. I listen to gospel on my commute if I do not have any other pressing issues.

- Use hands-free calling to get a head start on critical, time-sensitive issues. Personally, I use this time to call a willful parent to inform them that I am looking forward to our scheduled meeting. This sets a positive tone, as the parent is not expecting you to give them an early morning call. Additionally, they will not be able to comprehend that you are excited about the meeting; however, ultimately, they will realize that you made them and their child a priority, because you took your commute time to ensure they knew that you were thinking about them and their child.

- Send an inspirational text message to your teachers, students, and parents. Set a reminder in your phone to do this once a week, once a month, or as needed. *Remind 101* is a fantastic way to connect with your stakeholders.

- If you use public transit, or ride share programs, use the time to read and respond to emails.

- Call your mentor, or a family member, or a friend who will encourage you. Often, as leaders, we wait until our well is dry before we try to replenish ourselves. Your morning commute is an excellent way to charge yourself.

As an instructional leader, you should usually be the third person to your school building—third only to your lead custodian or principal. And each day that you arrive, expect to be met with an unforeseen issue—whether it be from the custodian, or a teacher, a staff member, a student, or a parent. And if it's a Monday or a Friday—be prepared for everyone mentioned in the scenario. Therefore, each day—you must be prepared; you must have an abundance of positive energy. As an assistant principal, it is imperative to ensure you are in good spirits, because everyone will take their cues from you. Allow your positive energy to be contagious. You should be their source of power and energy when theirs wanes.

The Significance of the Assistant Principal

> "Wake up early and tackle the day before it tackles you. Be on offense, not defense."
>
> ~ Evan Carmichael

Essential 3:

Arrive Early and Be Prepared to Be the Principal

Whether you are an assistant principal; assistant; instructional coach, or aspiring teacher leader during the school year, your schedule is overflowing with important responsibilities. One of the best ways to manage these responsibilities effectively is to focus on meeting students' needs and exceling at your job. This can be accomplished by one, simple change: each day, arrive to work at least a half hour early. Let's look at the key benefits of starting your workday early and why the assistant principal should be prepared to be the principal.

Less Stress

There's nothing more stressful that arriving to work late. More often than not, professionals either arrive on time, or a few minutes before the official clock in time. Again—we are professionals. Many of us know that, *to be early is to be on time. To be on time is to be late, and to be late is totally unacceptable.* You can save yourself a lot of undue stress, if you wake up earlier, and arrive to work earlier. There will be less traffic, and you will have more time to decide the type of day that you want to have. It is up to you whether you want to have an erratic day, or a productive day. If you could give yourself an advantage, by maximizing your time—why would you not do it? After all—you want to be viewed as a professional, correct? Your work arrival time can be a sure indicator of your professionalism, as well as indicative of whether you are eligible for a promotion. Seize the day by preparing for any unknowns in advance—this is a natural stress reducer, and it will help you to have a more productive day.

Gradually Ease into the Day
Most professionals barely make it to work on time, and even if they are not late, they leave little to no time to prepare for the day that lies ahead. As a result, they will begin the day flustered, and end the day exhausted. However, this does not have to be your reality. Gradually ease into your day. You may want to enjoy a cup of coffee or tea at your desk, while listening to your favorite song—before the hustle and bustle of the day begins. Conversely, you may use your time to

fine-tune your daily schedule—*Do you have a plan to meet all your deadlines? What are your three priorities for your day? Did you schedule all your meetings, and communicate with everyone who needs to attend?* If you did not—it's ok. Relax. You have extra time, now. You can begin your day in a relaxed state, verses a frenzied one. Taking the time to plan accordingly for the knowns and unknowns sets the tone for productivity and success.

You Are Always on Stage
Regardless of whether they say anything, your supervisors, your colleagues, and your students notice what time you report to work. Essentially, you are always on stage. They notice your patterns, and these consistent patterns speak to your professionalism, or lack thereof. If you arrive early, you will impress those who have been watching you—and you will never have to say a word; your actions will speak for you. Being early conveys your dedication to the profession; your actions will inspire others. As the assistant principal, you will set the tone for professionalism in your building (as well as your principal). Your arrival time can positively or negatively impact the culture in your building. If you are an assistant principal, your supervisor will know that you are dependable, and the

teachers and support staff that you manage will take your expectations of timeliness seriously. If you are an aspiring principal, your supervisors will take notice, and new opportunities will avail themselves to you. *The early bird gets the worm.* If you are on a grade-level team, or a member of a department—your colleagues will notice and match your actions.

Create A Culture of Calmness
How do you feel when you barely clock in on time? When you clock in late? Multiply these feelings by ten…by twenty…by thirty. Each person carries their own unique energy. The average school has a minimum of 100-150 faculty and staff members. On average, ten percent of the faculty and staff are chronically late. That's ten to fifteen people every day; five days a week—running late, hiding from their supervisors, and asking others to cover their morning duty. You see them—running for the sign-in clock, for the elevator, for the door, in hopes of making their tardiness disappear. This energy permeates throughout the work environment. It can stagnate a struggling culture and diminish a thriving culture. Coworkers who are on time become resentful of those who are frequently absent or tardy—especially if that person is an instructional, or aspiring leader. However, if

tardiness can damage a culture, imagine how the converse can affect the culture. If you make the commitment to arrive to work early, this means you won't bring frazzled energy into the workplace. You will be doing a service to everyone else who enters the space, from teachers and administrators—to students and visitors. When you and your colleagues feel at ease, it is easier to work in tandem towards common goals and objectives. Early arrival is at the helm of productivity.

Work-Life Balance
Most educators wake up when it is dark and depending on one's position in this profession—most educators do not return home until it is dark again. By then, there is little to no time to do anything for yourself, or for your family. Most educators go home and continue working (thinking about work)—neglecting self and all others. As a result, educators become prime candidates for stress and stress-related diseases. We find ourselves taking medication for high blood pressure; high cholesterol; anxiety, as well as for sleep. Cortisol is a hormone that is secreted into one's bloodstream to help regulate bodily functions; however, if one is stressed—the body secretes additional cortisol. Cortisol leads to increased health

concerns that create underlying health issues. Managing your stress level can and will have a positive impact on your health, as well as your productivity.

As educators, we are saddled with various ailments, because we do not practice what we preach to our parents, colleagues, and students. We tout the importance of a work-life balance to everyone—for everyone, but we do not advocate the same for ourselves. An earlier than usual rising will allow you to start your workday with more focus and momentum. Also, you will have more time to eat a healthy breakfast, meditate, or to devote time to a spiritual practice. If you begin your day earlier, you must commit to end your day earlier. This will afford you an opportunity to get some physical activity—whether you hit the gym for a workout, or you hit the pavement for a brisk walk, you should spend thirty minutes a day at an intentional, physical activity. This can become your me time—a time that is set aside just for you. By adopting a healthier lifestyle, you will effortlessly enhance your performance at work, and you will build your stamina to be able to conquer all the challenges during the day. Additionally, you will still have the energy to support your needs, or your family's needs when you return home.

Better—Not Bitter

If you rise early, you can retire to bed earlier. When was the last time you had eight, uninterrupted hours of sleep? Most educators function on four to six hours of sleep. This is unhealthy for so many reasons. Our brains need to rest, and our cells need time to rejuvenate. Inadequate sleep is almost analogous to a perpetual late start, and this leads to bitterness and lack of productivity. Therefore, getting an adequate amount of sleep is imperative to starting your day in an unhurried state. This slight adjustment to your schedule will improve your mood, and it will enhance your ability to focus. Instead of bringing stressed, frenetic energy at the onset of your day, you will be in a better position to focus clearly on each task that lies ahead of you.

The Educational Benefits of Relaxation

When you are relaxed, and in an optimal frame of mind, you naturally perform at your best. This will translate into doing your job more effectively, and you will be more centered. If you are an instructional leader—the entire staff will thrive because of your more focused state of being.

Most people dislike the feeling of being rushed during their commute and arriving to work with little time to spare. Resolve to avoid this feeling and all the stresses it creates by getting to work at least a half hour early every day. Whether you are an administrator or a teacher, everyone can benefit from getting to work early. Regardless of your position, if you arrive to work earlier, you will enjoy your job more, and your colleagues, your parents, and your students will feel the benefits as well. Instructional leaders—consider this: *If your teachers were happier, how would this impact student achievement?* I posit that if teachers are happier, they will be more apt to teach their students depth as well as breadth—and their students will be receptive.

Be Prepared to Be the Principal

There's one thing that you can be assured of as an assistant principal and that is there will be an event or events that will occur every day that will throw your day in a frenzy. However, if the principal is out the day can be chaotic. The position of the assistant principal is to assist the principal administratively, manage the schools, and be an effective instructional leader.

Assistant principals spend much of their time on managerial functions (e.g., textbooks, resources, equipment, and schedules), student discipline, student attendance, and student activities. While these tasks are important, there are many other roles assistant principals need to experience to hone their skills. Some of these are:

- Strategic planning
- School leadership
- Instructional leadership
- Human resources management
- Budgets and financial resources
- Partnerships with district administration and the school board
- Communication and public relations with the school community
- Legal Compliance

Expanding assistant principals' roles to provide experience in leadership ensures better preparation for the principal position. This is important as one day without any notice the assistant principal will receive a call from informing them that their principal will not be in for the day or out for the day, weeks, or months.

Partnering with the principal and shadowing the principal are two ways assistant principals can gain leadership experiences. The assistant principal should be knowledgeable of all components of the school as if they were the principal. Some critical areas are:

- The principal's daily and weekly schedule
- Important Initiatives
- Community Meetings
- The location of important documents
- Parents they have been dealing with
- Discussion they have had with teachers or grade levels

Having a deep understanding of each of these areas a critical, because one day you will be the principal when you're least expected and you must be prepared.

The Significance of the Assistant Principal

"I like to greet anyone who comes to my house with a lot of positivity and peace."

~ Adnan Sami

Essential 4:

Greet Every Student and Staff Member

The morning greeting—it is the most important part of an assistant principal's day. When possible, the assistant principal should greet every student, teacher, and staff member with a genuine *"Good morning!"* For some students and staff alike—this will be the only greeting he or she receives. *"Good morning! How are you?"* You are going to have an awesome and amazing day! This is my morning greeting to everyone as they enter the building. And for good measure, for my students—I add my famous fist bump. This verbal and physical connection allows me to not only give each person a warm welcome, but also observe and note who may be having a rough morning, and thus be in need of additional inspiration, or support for a few minutes before going into the classroom.

As an assistant principal, being the first, or second person in your building has its benefits. You will see it all, and you will be able to respond appropriately—if you are there. The angry parent who's walking fast to the office, poised to make a scene—intercept them. De-escalate the situation and listen to understand—not just to respond. The teacher who's crying, and quickly drying her face on the way in—intercept her, and direct her to your office, and your bathroom as you continue to go through your morning ritual of being visible—being present. The student whose mother yelled at him before he left home—you will see his budding rage, and his sadness—his embarrassment. Let him stand with you after you greet him until he is calm…until he feels seen and heard. Do not send him into the learning environment when his basic need for security and a sense of belonging have not been met. The paraprofessional who is battling cancer, slowly making her way to the door—if you are comfortable, hug her, and thank her for being dedicated to you, to the students, and to the profession. Your loyal, front desk administrative assistant who shows up, despite her doctor's orders telling her to stay home with her feet elevated. As you see her making her way in—give her your best *picture day smile* and remind her that her health is important to you. Offer to work the front for a moment—when she returns, tell her how grateful you are that she is in the position. The coach who had a late game, lost, but ensured every player made it home safely. Give him a pound—*That was a good game last night, Coach! I know we'll pull a dub at the next game.* This is a critical time to recognize and address issues that can easily change the trajectory of your day.

Deliver an Inspirational Morning Message

The Significance of the Assistant Principal

As the assistant principal you will have an experience with troubled students every day. Every indicator will indicate there's no hope for these students. However, your words, reaction to their social-emotional needs, and response during these interactions will either fuel or extinguish their flame of hope and possibilities.

-Dr. Marcus D. Jackson

Essential 5:

Visit Your Students, Teachers and Conduct Positive Walkthroughs

After the morning announcements, it is important to visit your students, teachers, and conduct positive walkthroughs. If there is a parent waiting for you, they will have to wait. Every teacher needs to be visited and given a genuine, *good morning!* And a warm-hearted, *Have an awesome day!* The power of positive thinking and greetings is a popular concept that can sometimes feel a little cliché. But the physical and mental benefits of positive thinking have been demonstrated by multiple scientific studies.

These daily visits and personal greetings reinforced the caring culture that an assistant principal should strive to establish and to maintain. Teachers and students need to see that the administrators are on the same page. Positive affirmations and greetings are essential. Disgruntled adults and unhappy children should not gain a foothold in the building. When teachers and students know that the educational leaders would be around to greet them—many negative attitudes changed to positive, and off-task behavior became a distant practice. Furthermore, this is an excellent way to build your team's capacity. Finally, by collecting this qualitative and quantitative data, you can build up your team when they are weary. Debrief to discuss the positives. *Wow! We visited 42 classrooms, and 40 of them were enthusiastic and engaging! Our numbers are steadily increasing, team! Thank you for your positive impact on our teachers and students! We are creating a caring culture, where adults want to collaborate, and children want to learn!* You will need this good feeling—because lunch, a potential time for mischief, is right around the corner.

The assistant principalship is a challenging and stressful job. However, all that changed with an encounter with a second-grade student. After three major incidents in one day, involving fighting, sexual abuse, and child abuse—the energy level was gone. The student that was in the office heard the sigh and mentioning, this has been a crazy day—*an absolutely crazy day!* Immediately, the student responded, *Dr. Jackson, you're wrong! Today was a good day. You're looking at it wrong, Dr. J.!* He began to list the day's accomplishments that he took note of while he sat in the office during a lengthy, and much-needed time out. *I did all my work, Dr. Jackson! And you had three big things to happen, but it's ok—it's a lot of us kids that go to this school.* As he spoke, the thoughts changed—at that time there were over 800 students at the school, one assistant principal, and one instructional coach. He prattled on, as second graders will. *Good stuff happens more than bad stuff, but you can't see it, 'cause the bad stuff comes to your office. But you gotta pay attention to the good stuff, too, Dr. J.* Talk about…*out of the mouths of babes…* He was right, and that was the last day, leaving work feeling exhausted, frustrated, and overwhelmed.

A positive mindset can give you more confidence, improve your mood, and even reduce the likelihood of developing conditions such as hypertension, depression and other stress-related disorders. All this sounds great, but what does the power of positive thinking really mean? You can define positive thinking as positive imagery, positive self-talk, or general optimism, but these are all still generalized, ambiguous concepts, because they rely solely on the perceiver. If you want to master the art of positivity, you will need concrete examples to avoid vagueness.

A second grader helped me to change my mindset. I always thought of myself as a positive person, but after the motivational speech that my student gave me, I decided to be more intentional about my positive outlook—personally and professionally. One of the first personal changes that I made was to write my own mantras—I taped them to my mirror, and to my bedside table. I say them before I go to sleep, when I awake, and I practice positive self-talk throughout the day. My major professional change was to begin my day with positive walkthroughs. During my positive walkthroughs, there are ten areas I focus on:

First Impressions—The Face of the Front Office
Your front office administrative assistant is one of the most influential people in your building. Your front office is a hub. In most buildings, everyone passes through the front office in the morning to sign in; it tends to be the place where students or teachers go when there is an emergency. Additionally, it is the primary check-in place for parents, district administration, and other stakeholders. This central location is where the first impressions about your building come to fruition for all your stakeholders. As the principal, you ensure that your front office is

aesthetically pleasing and inviting—matching décor, vibrant colors, plants, etc. Yet, how much time do you spend to ensure that your front office person is a true representation of your school's mission and vision? It is imperative for the front office personnel to be smiling, to be kind, and to have an innate, calm spirit. Your front office staff will be the first person that many people encounter; his/her daily mood and interactions with teachers, students, parents, and other stakeholders is critical to the community's perception of your school.

First Impressions—The Building
A clean school is one of the most important components in creating a thriving, positive learning environment. Consider how you feel when you walk into a clean restaurant verses a dirty restaurant. At which restaurant are you more inclined to eat—to revisit? The same is true for your school—first impressions are lasting impressions. Your faculty, staff, and students deserve a clean environment that is conducive to learning. Ensure that your administrators are aware of your expectations as it relates to the cleanliness and aesthetics of the school. Be clear about how you expect the school and its environs to look, smell, and feel. Communicate this same message to

your custodial staff as well. Charge them to be vigilant, but also empower them to bring suggestions to you that will promote cleanliness and safety. Ensure that they know they are an integral part of your dream team.

People Are Present

As common sense suggests, teacher attendance is directly related to student outcomes—the more teachers are absent, the more their students' achievement suffers. When teachers are absent ten days or more, the decrease in student achievement is significant. It is synonymous with having a brand-new teacher, or a teacher with one to two years of experience. Moreover, studies show a disproportionately high rate of teacher absenteeism in schools serving low income and minority students; this is yet another obstacle to closing the achievement gap. Along this same vein—you want your students to be present as well—teachers' acumen becomes ineffective when students are frequently absent. Expect to have a pocket of students who have barriers to consistent attendance and strive to be proactive to overcome these barriers. How do you acknowledge the professionalism of your faculty and staff who show up every day—ahead of schedule? What student incentives are in place to promote consistent attendance? Engage your parent liaison and other school leaders to discuss how to convey the importance of adult and student attendance.

The Assistant Principal's Role—One of Many

The assistant principal is as important to the school as the respiratory system is to the body. As the assistant principal, you are responsible for establishing and maintaining a culture of positive energy, excitement, and enthusiasm for learning throughout the school. All vital information should come through the principal. Everyone should align their values with that of the principal, so that the corps can move in unison. As principal, while it is important for you to have a finger on the pulse of the school—you must also remember that ultimately, you are the heart and soul of the school. Therefore, ensure that you do a self-check every day. How is your attitude? What do your facial expressions convey? Are you actively listening? Are you treating everyone fairly? What does your body language convey when one of your staff members is not performing optimally? Check your tone as well. More often than not—it is not what we say, but how we say it. As a reflective practitioner, ensure that you model the professional behavior that you expect from your faculty and staff. Are you encouraging and supportive, or are you viewed as negative, and unwilling to help? Your faculty, staff, and students must be comfortable to approach you with any concern. You must be willing to sacrifice your ego daily, in order to be a servant leader to those who depend on you.

Instructional Support Is Positive

Instructional Support Services are designed to provide mandated, educational services to students with exceptionalities. If a child has been assigned an Individualized Education Plan (IEP), it must be followed to support the student's academic progress. As you are conducting your walks, do you see evidence of your special education teachers providing individualized instruction and support? Are your paraprofessionals actively engaged in the lesson? Are they providing the appropriate instructional support to their students? Is assistive technology being used appropriately? Do you see positive teacher-student interactions? Are your teachers frustrated, or are they encouraging? Are their students genuinely excited about being in the classroom?

In this same space, how is your instructional coach providing positive support to all teachers? Does he or she give positive, yet balanced feedback? Is he/she tactful, supportive, and willing to support everyone fairly? How are you building capacity in this individual?

Teachers Are Enthusiastic

It's imperative that teachers greet their students at the door. The teachers should show genuine enthusiasm for their students' arrival. This sets the tone for the day as students will emulate their teachers' positivity. An enthusiastic teacher makes learning exciting and enjoyable. Students are teeming with anticipation; they are engaged, and they are eager to explore more about the content.

Genuine teacher enthusiasm can lead to better evaluations; better student outcomes; mitigated off-task behavior, and collaborative, collegial relationships. Your teachers are a reflection of you. Empower them to create a positive learning environment that is conducive to learning. What is their belief about students' ability to learn, retain, and apply new information? Why do they want to teach at your school? Do they feel that they have purpose? Do they feel valued? What positive affirmations are they sharing with their students daily? What positive messages are they communicating to the parents, to their colleagues, and to you? Two of the most reflective questions we can ask ourselves as educators are— *Would I want to be a student in this classroom? Would I want my child to be a student in this classroom?* If the answers are yes—excellent job! If not, triage the situation immediately.

Students Are Ready to Learn

Students should be prepared to learn in all their classes. If their teachers have given them clear, succinct instructions, you should see students…

- Seated, with all necessary materials (pen; pencil; paper; laptop, etc.)
- Working on an independent, engaging activity that primes them for the day's lesson.
- Following protocols and procedures, independent of the teacher.
- Focused, and persevering to complete the assigned task.

Students Are Actively Engaged

Research has proven that engaging students in the learning process increases their attention focus and motivates them to practice higher-level, critical thinking skills. Teachers can promote meaningful learning experiences, while simultaneously improving student engagement by:

- Removing unnecessary barriers.
- Giving students voice and choice.
- Activating prior knowledge first, then connecting it to content.
- Providing authentic, specific, relevant, frequent feedback.
- Creating multiple opportunities to stimulate the various learning modalities.

Students Are Well-behaved, and Teachers Are Encouraging

There are a handful of characteristics found in effective classrooms that every teacher should work towards cultivating. These features set managerial, behavioral, and instructional guidelines—for teachers and students alike—that help to preemptively solve problems. A few of these characteristics are:

- Student engagement.

- Clear expectations for learning.
- Use of a timer to support effective time management.
- Positive work environment that promotes risk-taking, and rewards creativity.
- Firm, fair policies that are aligned to the district's progressive, systemic approach to discipline.

Teachers and Students Are Cordial

Authentic, teacher-student interactions are at the heart of every model classroom. Genuine, daily greetings let your students know that you care about them, not only as students, but as people, too. By starting the day on a positive note—such as a warm greeting, students will feel valued, and they will be happier about coming to school, and to your class. They will approach learning with a growth mindset. This small, genuine act is the foundation to establishing and maintaining appropriate, authentic teacher-student relationships. This connection is vital for learning. Students will work to impress their teachers if they know their teachers care about their futures.

Deliver an Inspirational Morning Message

Positive Walkthrough Observations	
First Impressions: *The Face of the Front Office* Tallies: Comments:	First Impressions: *The Building* Tallies: Comments:
People Are Present Tallies: Comments:	The Principal's Role—One of Many Tallies: Comments:
Instructional Support is Positive Tallies: Comments:	Teachers Are Enthusiastic Tallies: Comments:
Students Are Ready to Learn Tallies: Comments:	Students Are Actively Engaged Tallies: Comments:
Students Are Well-behaved & Teachers Are Enthusiastic Tallies: Comments:	Teachers & Students Are Cordial Tallies: Comments:

Use tally marks on the *Positive Walkthrough* Observations to document your observations, or make comments as needed. Make note of *Glows and Grows*.

Visit Your Students

As an assistant principal, your office will become a revolving door with a plethora of students having behavioral, academically, and social-emotional issues. During the time in your office, students will become very comfortable with you. Through discussion and dialogue, you will be able to discover the root cause of behavioral and academic deficiencies. Additionally, you will be exposed to their strengths and special talents. For example, a student beating on their desk with their pencil is an indicator that you may have a future drummer on your hand, a student who is allowed to color to calm down and you notice is coloring is perfect, this may be an indicator of artistic talent, or the student you ask him to write his teacher and apology letter and his writing is spectacular even with his grammatical errors. This may be a future author. These special talents are thing you will notice about these students as they will consistently referred to the office.

These students will eventually become **your** students. Therefore, it's imperative to circle back as you visit teachers and conduct your positive walkthroughs. These students will be seeking your love as they will be approach you while greeting teachers and conducting positive walkthroughs and they will be crushed if you're unable to give them some of your attention.

When you meet with **your** students, there are a few things you must do:

1.) Ask them how are they doing?
2.) Tell them that you are proud of them
3.) Let the know you will try to check back in on them and you are expecting them to have a great day behaviorally and academically.
4.) Finish the meeting with a special fist bump designed specifically for them

The Significance of the Assistant Principal

You have a choice. You can run the day, or the day can run you. If you properly plan, you can prevent a plethora of problems.

~Dr. Marcus D. Jackson

Essential 6:

Morning Meeting with Your Principal

The morning meeting with your principal is critical to ensuring that your day is effective and efficient. This meeting must be short brief and very intentional. This meeting must focus on five things. These things are:

1.) Wellness Check – ask them how are they doing mentally and physically? During this time principals will tell you they are fine. This is how they are wired. It's important to read their body language if the discussion need to be extended. Also, it is important for you to be vulnerable.

2.) Take something off their plate – a principal can have an email, irate parent, or visitor from the district office that can throw their entire schedule off. Therefore, it's imperative to ask what you can take off their plate.

3.) Fill them in on yesterday's concerns and issues – a principal's worst nightmare is to be caught off guard with an incident that they were not aware of. During your morning meeting, it's important to mention situation you're handling with parents, suspensions, concerns from teachers, and any other concern you may have of the daily operations of the school.

4.) Review Instructional Support Schedule – this is when you and your principal will share your instructional support schedule. During this time, you will discuss common themes you're seeing amongst teachers each of you have visited and common areas of refinement. It is important to stick to your instructional support schedule.

Example of Weekly Instructional Support Schedule
Week Of _____

Monday
8:00a–8:45a
Observations (Lewis, Cohen, Davis, Brown)
Focus _____

10:15a-11:00a
Team Teaching (McKinney & Clark)

Tuesday
8:00a–8:45a
Small Group (6 students–Gray & Laury)

10:15a–11:00a
Model Lesson (Peterson)

Wednesday
8:00a–8:45a
Observations (Miller, Perrymond, Gilbert-Jackson)
Focus_____

10:15a–11:00a
Team Teaching (Jones & Jackson)

Thursday
8:00a–8:45a
Small Group (6 students–Johnson & Lewis)

10:15a–11:00a
Model Lesson (Taylor)

Friday
8:00a–8:45a
Observations (Art, Music, Physical Education, & Technology)

Focus _____

10:15a–11:00a
Special Education Observations (Collaborative & Small Group)
Focus _____

Essential 7:

Live in the Organizational Framework: Know all Master Two

COLA-C ® Organizational Framework

As an assistant principal, remember—every success and every failure is a direct result of your leadership, or lack thereof. In my years as principal, I developed an organizational framework that supported and sustained all facets of my schools. I am sharing it with you; use it to garner the results that you want to see in your building. This is a powerful instrument to build capacity in your current and aspiring leaders.

Therefore, as the principal, it is imperative that you select the members of each committee. If you are a veteran administrator in your building, you should know the strengths of your faculty and staff members. If you are a newly-appointed principal, then rely on your administrative team to help with selection, and the delegation of duties. Ensure that you appoint faculty and staff members who will be willing to collaborate—to strive together to meet common goals. This organizational framework will touch every aspect of your school, so, it is necessary to consider the commitment of the members of each team. The team should have clear duties and responsibilities. Additionally, your school's mission, vision, and year-long goals should drive the work of the committees.

COLA-C®

COLA-C® is a comprehensive system that
is implemented during our leadership academy. This integrated system is designed to ensure that there are clear expectations for key areas. By implementing these systems, you will minimize confusion, and maintain homeostasis.

Curriculum

Members of the Curriculum team typically include content chairs, and the instructional coach. This team is charged with ensuring the fidelity of the curriculum in each content. Further, the team is responsible for brainstorming, suggesting, and implementing programs that support acceleration and remediation, in relation to high stakes testing. Some key foci are writing across the curriculum; school-wide vocabulary plan; lesson plan components; end caps (bulletin boards) schedule, and the academic gallery board.

The duties and responsibilities of the Curriculum team include, (but do not have to be limited to,) understanding the State Standards of Excellence. This team will be responsible for deconstructing standards to create learning targets, that are written in student-friendly language. These learning targets are the crux of a well-planned lesson. This committee can also review lesson plans and determine the key foci of said plans. Additionally, they will also assist with developing common assessments. It is crucial for your team to have a deep understanding of fielding questions that align to the lesson and unit standards, as well as the lessons' learning targets. Further, this group will set a schedule for, and monitor collaborative planning in your building.

Operations & Logistics

Members of the Operations & Logistics team typically include your *gold* faculty members—those who thrive on order, policies, and procedures. This team is charged with ensuring that the daily operations are communicated. They are responsible for creating systems and protocols for campus safety and security, arrival and dismissal procedures, school-wide routines, and bell schedules. Additionally, this team works in tandem with administration to develop school-wide discipline expectations, surrounding ISS; office referrals; dress code implementation and infractions; faculty/staff handbook, and the creation of morning and afternoon duty rosters.

The Operations & Logistics team will be responsible for ensuring your building runs like a well-oiled machine—even in your absence. These professionals will monitor attendance; the school's weekly and master calendar; create and communicate school-wide functions, and brainstorm school fundraisers. Additionally, this committee will create a flowchart or an FAQ to support the age-old question, *where do I go if I need...?* Also, the O & L team will create a system for custodial, maintenance, and furniture requests to mitigate replication, and to support efficiency.

Achievement

The Achievement team members are responsible for working in tandem with administration to create the School Improvement Plan; disaggregating formative, summative, and high-stakes achievement data.

Additionally, this team needs to have a shared belief about the importance of strong, cross-curricular literacy initiatives. They will be responsible for educating the faculty and staff about *Lexiles*; creating a system to gauge and monitor student *Lexiles* by grade level, as well as suggesting research-based literacy strategies to raise student *Lexiles*. This work is paramount, as literacy affects every domain of student learning. Student literacy is an area that often gets overlooked. If you want to see exponential student growth and achievement in your building, spend some time around understanding *Lexiles*.

Also, this team will be responsible for creating, and updating a school-wide data room; creating common assessments creating a system for progress monitoring; assisting in the RTI/SST process; monitoring and supporting initiatives to augment the graduation rate; implementing academic and behavioral interventions, and establishing a viable, school-wide incentive program. This group will also recognize *Students of the Month*, help with new teacher orientation, and establish and maintain a robust, student mentor program.

Culture & Climate Team

This highly functioning team is responsible for creating and maintaining a positive school culture. While the main goal is to bolster and maintain faculty, staff, and student morale, this group of professionals will also be responsible for other functions that can positively impact your school's climate. This group will organize off-site gatherings; shore up peer-to-peer, and teacher-to-student relationships; recognize birthdays, organize equitable celebrations, and create and maintain a *Sunshine Fund* to be used for celebrations—weddings; newborns; degree completion, etc., as well as funeral donations.

Because this team will also touch areas of academics, by infusing cultural relevance into lessons, it is suggested that the members complete cultural competency training. Additionally, they will be responsible for peer evaluation schedules and procedures; faculty mentor/mentee program; creating a schedule for leadership team meetings; updating the school's website, and most importantly building and maintaining efficacious relationships. Remember—*Everyone has a penny, a nickel, or a dime to contribute to the quarter of success.*

> *The Significance of the Assistant Principal*
>
> Having an organizational system for accepting phone calls, returning phone call, answering, and responding to emails is necessary to ensure you communicate effectively and reach you optimal level.
>
> *--Dr. Marcus D. Jackson*

Essential 8:

Establish an Extinguishing System

Any fires from the previous day or the new day, must be extinguished, because rest assured—more are on the way. Here's how to be proactive, rather than reactive. Create a system to deal with these fires, so they do not rage out of control. I use a color-coded, filing system. You can use colored folders, trays, or even stickers. Ensure that you share your system with every leader in your building, so that they understand your communication, and your expectations.

Anything that is *Urgent*, goes in my Red Folder. For me, an urgent deadline is something that needs to be addressed in a few hours—before the end of the day. It does not matter who the task is from, but rather *when* it needs to be addressed. This could include a response to a *helicopter parent*; my immediate supervisor; a follow-up conversation; a PDP deadline, etc. I have the autonomy to decide what is urgent. In the same folder—I mentally include the 4 B's. These take precedence over everything. *My baby*—I am a father first. My boss. A directive can immediately change the course of my day. *The boys in blue.* If the police are in my building, or if there is a lockdown—I stop everything to address the immediate threat. And finally—*my Boo.* Sometimes, emergencies can arise in our personal lives that need our immediate attention. Additionally, if my administrative assistant, or one of my instructional leaders need me to address something immediately, he or she knows to code the message *Red*—if they need a response before the end of the day.

If something *needs to be addressed* today—by the end of the day, it goes in my Yellow Folder. A *Yellow* task, while pressing, is not as urgent as a *Red* task. However, a *Yellow* task does carry its own bit of gravity. Examples of *Yellow* tasks, ironically, can be the same ones that I used for the *Red Folder.* The difference in importance can solely depend on the relationship that you have with the originator of the task, or it can be the amount of time and resources that it will take for you to complete the task. If it is urgent, but you need more time, and you have the flexibility, place it in your *Yellow Folder.* Another example of a *Yellow* task may be fulfilling a promise to go and teach one of your teacher's classes. This is an amazing way to stay connected to your faculty, staff, and students.

Finally, if something needs to be addressed within 24-48 hours, it goes in my *Green Folder*. An example of a *Green Folder* message may be completing a recommendation for a colleague, or for a student; attending a meeting with my parent liaison; following up with the instructional support that my instructional coach is providing to my novice and struggling teachers. None of these examples are etched in stone—you have the autonomy to move your tasks around—even if one of your coworkers has placed them elsewhere. However, in these instances, ensure you communicate with the originator, so that you fully understand why he or she marked something *Urgent*. Communication is key for this system to work—I know many of us rely on our calendar for updates, but I also know that technology—at any time, can fail. Also—when tasks are *hidden*—like on a calendar, it is easy to forget the amount of work that it will take to accomplish the task. The folder system works for me—even if it is not for you, use it to build the capacity of your leaders. Let them implement the system, and give them tasks and scenarios, and guide them to what should go where, based on your experience.

Overall, remember to include your administrative team. You may have a fifteen-minute check in meeting in the mornings to discuss what your priorities are for the day. Ask what's in their folders and ask if they need support. Moreover, ensure that priorities are addressed as early as possible in the morning. Once you extinguish your *Red Folder* flames—take a quick breath—there are coals smoldering elsewhere, and they will most assuredly burst into flames…probably during your third lunch, when you are short-staffed, and your supervisor drops in for an unannounced visit. However, you will not have to stress, because you have a system in place to address the little fires.

Establish an Extinguishing System

The Significance of the Assistant Principal

If you want to lead, you must serve.
If you serve, you must be transparent.
If you are transparent, you must be honest.
If you are honest, you must be reflective.
If you are reflective, you must be resilient.
If you are resilient, you must be trustworthy.
If you are trustworthy, you must be patient.
If you are patient, you must have faith.
If you have faith, you must be willing to see the impossible.
If you can see the impossible, you must be willing to go further.
If you want to lead, you must follow.
You must follow your dreams. You must fulfill your destiny.
You must be willing to accept that others are depending on you.
If you want to lead, you must lead with integrity, graciousness, boldness, and courage.
If you want to lead, you must be all things to all people, so that your faculty, staff, and students can reach their full potential.

--Dr. Marcus D. Jackson

Essential 9:

Make Your Instructional Presence Felt: Cycle of Academic Excellence

The Conceptual Framework Cycle of Academic Excellence is a research-based approach to provide support to teachers to ensure their effectiveness and efficiency.

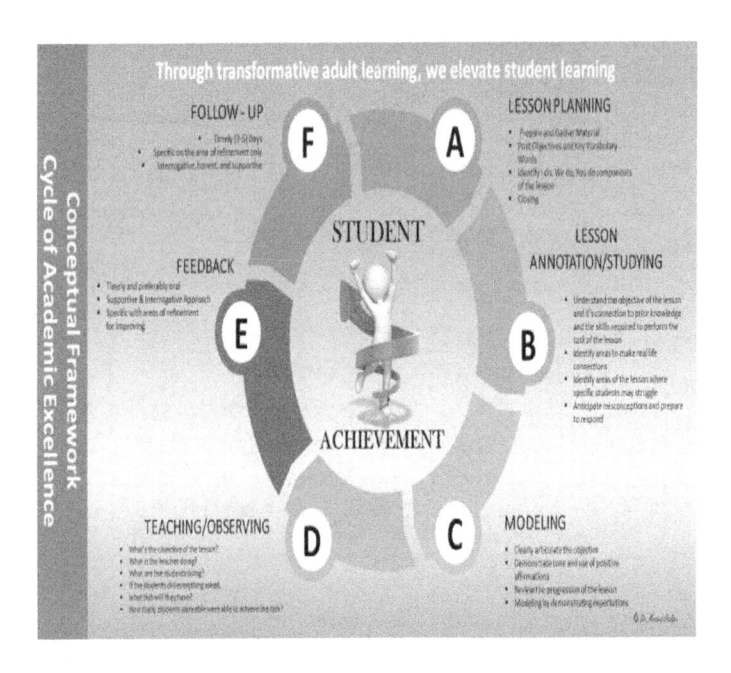

The Cycle of Academic Excellence—A: Lesson Planning Tool

What is the purpose of lesson planning? It helps the teacher demonstrate their skills, intelligence, and personality. Just as students need structure, teachers do, too. Lesson planning helps with organization and avoids repetition where it is not warranted. Because teachers submit plans in advance, you and your instructional team will be able to review the plans and provide teachers with meaningful feedback. This will ensure that plans are aligned to district initiatives, as well as your instructional expectations. Further, as the instructional leaders, you can pinpoint who needs private support, and public praise.

Further, if there is a robust, succinct system in place that supports effective lesson planning, then you will begin to see an uptick in teacher and student efficacy, as well as achievement. Teachers can be reflective and candid about their practice. With a rigorous lesson plan in place, the instructor is better prepared, and students are more apt to succeed.

During weekly planning, instructors should prepare and gather materials for the week's lesson; determine key vocabulary words, and identify the *I*

Do, We Do, and *You Do* components of the lesson. A good lesson plan for all grade levels contains the following:

I Do

Goals and Objectives

In this section, the teacher shares the lesson focus. He or she must share the lesson's goals and objectives; this gives students a specific destination. It ensures them that there is a focus to the lesson, and that there are obtainable objectives and an overall goal. Further, the teacher explicitly shows the students how to work towards proficiency.

The teacher must have clearly defined, overarching goals that align to current, educational standards. By defining goals in advance, the instructor will be able to determine what students should be able to accomplish by the end of the unit, and how they will show mastery of the material. To ensure clarity, and scale, the goals should be broad; however, the objectives should be **SMART** (**S**pecific, **M**easurable, **A**ttainable, **R**elevant, and **T**ime-bound).

Anticipation and Background Knowledge

When teachers stimulate anticipation, and probe for background knowledge, they foster a sense of excitement by piquing their students' interest. By tapping into what their students already know, they value their students' knowledge and experiences, while simultaneously providing a context for learning. This approach ensures instructor preparation, as well as priming, so that students can absorb and relate to the lesson.

Direct Instruction

This is where the teacher does all the heavy lifting, as it is the main part of the lesson. New concepts are introduced, and the lesson objectives are addressed. In this section, the teacher deconstructs the standards, shares learning objectives in student friendly language, while the students absorb the information. This part of the lesson may include showing examples of a key concept, displaying diagrams, or defining new vocabulary. The instructor should consider the students' learning styles to determine the approach to the lesson. This is paramount, as the students will mimic what the teacher did, as they work towards standards mastery.

We Do
In this part of the lesson, the instructor and students work together to process, understand, and develop the skills needed to move forward successfully. Here, the teacher continues to clarify misconceptions by answering questions, and modeling, if necessary.

Guided Practice
This is the part of the lesson plan where students will practice what they have learned. The teacher should design guided practice activities for students to work on in small groups or as a collective. The protocols and procedures for these activities should be explained during the direct instruction portion. These activities should be classified as cooperative or individual learning. In this part of the lesson, the teacher should practice aggressive monitoring to check for understanding. As he/she makes the monitoring rounds, he/she should verify students' correct answers, and clarify students' incorrect answers. This scaffolded support will lead to mastery of the objectives, as well as alleviate students' frustrations.

You Do
The last phase of the lesson involves empowering students to move on their own. This is where students

show what they know, without teacher intervention. At this point, they have been shown what to do, explicitly, and with support. Now is the time for them to be independent of the teacher, and of their peers.

Independent Practice
Students should have an opportunity to demonstrate what they learned. The lesson plan should include homework and other independent assignments, so the instructor, as well as the students, can gauge standards mastery. Independent practice is necessary, because it reinforces their individual skill set, and knowledge. If the lesson has been planned and executed correctly, students should be able to complete the tasks on their own.

Student success is contingent on a well-planned lesson. It is essential for teachers to have all their materials at the onset of the lesson to ensure proper time management, as he or she teaches. Along this same vein, the teacher must consider one of the most important parts of the lesson plan—assessment and follow-up. The instructor should administer an assessment that is aligned to the learning objectives. A teacher can assess formally or informally.

Closure
This section outlines the wrap-up of the lesson. While no new information needs to be introduced, it is acceptable to discuss additional concepts that may enhance meaning for the students. When the lesson is finished, students can organize and process the information they learned. The teachers should engage the students in a discussion to learn whether they mastered their learning objectives. Furthermore, though the goals are overarching, the students can still explain their understanding of the goals. Closing the lesson is imperative in order to validate the students' learning. An unclosed lesson is as valuable as a penny with a hole in it.

The Cycle of Academic Excellence—B: Lesson Annotation/Studying

Prior to a PLC, instructors annotate and study their lesson to understand fully the material that they will teach their students. These professional practices help teachers customize the lesson based on their students, and their classroom environment. An annotated lesson plan also prepares the instructor and provides him or her with the tools needed to teach on standard—not just on topic. Additionally, teachers build their own confidence in meeting state standards, and they can determine the needs of their students.

During the PLC, teachers practice various parts of their lesson in front of their colleagues. This way—if a teacher has any professional deficits or glaring strengths—they can receive feedback from their peers in a protected environment. Additionally, the co-teacher is present, so that his/her content knowledge is strengthened. Invite the co-teacher to share Specially Designed Instruction(al) (SDI) strategies that can and will benefit all. The goal is to identify areas where certain students may struggle and anticipate misconceptions that may arise. It is helpful if the co-teacher, and the teacher of record have a notebook (physical or electronic) that details each special education student's exceptionality. These must be taken into consideration as they plan. Teachers will annotate what Student A with Exceptionality B will be doing during specific portions of the lesson that may prove to be challenging for the student, based on his/her deficit. Furthermore, typically, the instructional coach, and or the content assistant principal are present to serve as a guide. Teachers will also think of the probing questions to be asked during the *Guided Practice* portion of the lesson.

An annotated lesson plan has the following:

Foundation

The foundation of a lesson plan is important, and it must be strong. Teachers can root their plans in the *What*, the *When*, and the *Why*. What will the students do? When will they do it? And why will they do it? Answering these questions will be key to executing the lesson. The instructor should annotate the key points of the lesson, and how those key points will translate into positive learning outcomes for their students. This foundation should also include the theoretical framework of the lesson plan objectives. A good rule of thumb is using an organizational format that has two columns. On the left side—the teacher should write notes on his/her actions, and the right side should denote student actions taken. This will ensure students remain actively engaged in the lesson.

Advanced Preparation

Instructors must prepare students, by drawing on their prior knowledge. Here, teachers outline what will be taught, and they pinpoint where certain students will have problems. Teachers state what alternative teaching strategies will be used to address these students' deficits. An example of advanced preparation is for teachers to deconstruct their standards, prior to the PLC. In doing so, the teacher will determine the key vocabulary that needs to be taught at the beginning of the lesson. The vocabulary should be tiered to allay any potential misconceived notions. This pre-work is a time-saver. Here's a suggestion: Have teachers to highlight the text in assorted colors to denote which words may be more difficult and may need deeper explanations. Depending on the students and their mode of learning, support can look like the use of visual aids, or even making a kinesthetic connection. An administrative look for, in reviewing the annotated lesson plan, is seeing the vocabulary explicitly stated and color-coded. Where the scaffolded support occurs is as important as the support itself.

Active Instruction

During this part of the lesson, the instructor should annotate what resources will be used and when. Additionally, if there is an accommodation, or a modification—this should be noted as well. Annotations should also include areas where students will collaborate. For example, students will use the *Think-Pair-Share* method to generate possible answers to the essential question.

While engaging in active instruction, teachers should consider the standards students are supposed to meet, as well as consider what probing questions can be asked to anticipate and clarify misconceptions. This is also where teachers will list appropriate learning outcomes that are aligned to students' abilities. Each learning target should be outlined, explaining how it relates to the lesson, and its relation to the standard to ensure compliance versus comfort.

Reflection

Reflection is key for all learners. Here, instructors consider a reflection question for their students, annotating what the question should achieve. For example: The reflection question will determine student acquisition of the learning objectives. Using the previously discussed two-sided chart, instructors should have key phrases to continue probing, noting which students responded and how they responded. This quantitative and qualitative data will support teachers' reflection in how their lessons were received. Additionally, it informs the teacher who needs more support, and who is ready to move on.

Evidence of Student Learning
The instructor should list the plan to evaluate student learning, based on performance indicators. The teacher may choose to assess formally or informally. However, assessment is paramount. This will provide information for further study, and it will uncover additional resources that some students may need.

The Cycle of Academic Excellence—C: Modeling
Modeling is an important and effective strategy. It shows students that the objectives and tasks can be independently completed. By continuously reviewing the lesson progression, and by demonstrating the expectations before handing them off to students, teachers help build confidence in every student. Most students thrive when they work to meet their instructors' expectations, and their peers strive to operate in the same spaces.

Unequivocally, anything instructors want their students to be able to do—should be modeled, explicitly. The primary goal of modeling is to prepare every student, so they will be successful if they are asked to demonstrate their understanding of the content. The overarching goal is for students to replicate the entire process from start to finish, visualizing each step along the way. Modeling engages students at a deeper, cognitive level, while proactively mitigating student error. Further, it also increases the probability of producing self-regulated learners, while shaping student-perception of the importance of the tasks.

So, what does an expertly modeled lesson plan look like? The teacher must state the lesson's objective(s), state what the students will learn by the end of the lesson and share the aligned assessment and task completion expectations.

Teachers must explain to the students how they should behave, or persist, as they engage in the lesson. For some lessons, this may mean demonstrating how to use applicable manipulatives, and materials, how to respond to a question, etc.

Teachers should welcome active, student engagement. They should allow students to participate in kinesthetic activities that support cognitive connections. Educators should maximize the power of small group discussions, whiteboards, and a chance system—such as pulling cards with student names to elicit responses; these research-based techniques should be methodically implemented to promote engagement, critical thinking, and independence.

Additionally, teachers should walk their classroom, as they aggressively monitor for understanding and engagement. During this time, teachers should also guide students to a definitive understanding by answering questions, probing students, reminding students of the concepts modeled, and allocating appropriate time to support the flow of activities. Also, this is an excellent time for teachers to compliment students' positive behavior. It is important to publicly praise a student who is on task, following directions, and going beyond what is expected. When the other students know why their peer is being recognized, they will strive to emulate their peer's behavior.

The Cycle of Academic Excellence—D: Teaching/Observing

Teaching and observing work in tandem. It is up to the instructor to determine the objective of the lesson, what he/she should be doing as an instructor, and how the students should be engaged. Instructors should be asking the following questions of themselves:

- Did the students take notes during Modeling, and refrain from questions?
- Did the students go through the Guided Practice with me?
- How many students were able to achieve the task during Guided Practice?
- Did students have too many questions during the Guided Practice? If so, did I return to the Modeling portion, before allowing the students to move forward?
- Did I verify and clarify students correct and incorrect answers to support efficacy and achievement?

One practice instructor should implement when observing their students is to look for signs of student frustration. While productive struggle is good, teachers need to know when their students have moved beyond a productive struggle to a heightened level of frustration. It is in this moment, that sitting beside them, having conversations, and asking probing questions can be one of the best techniques. Guide the students to their understanding, versus spoon-feeding them the answer. It is important to watch the process children use to master skills, content, and concepts. Formal and informal assessment are key. When assessing for student learning, instructors should strive to gain information from each student daily to inform their instruction. Assessment data should be created and graded for mastery.

Whenever possible, observe students through self-assessment. The instructor should provide opportunities for students to assess their efforts and the efforts of their peers. Students can use checklists, journaling, and questionnaires to accomplish this. Additionally, student portfolios are effective for students to set goals, and to gauge their benchmark achievements throughout the year. It is equally important to observe students individually and collectively. As an administrator, it is imperative that you have a systemic way for teachers to aggressively monitor their students, so that their data can be used to facilitate student achievement, as well as teacher efficacy. How much more effective is it for you to conduct a classroom observation, and you, too, have a copy of the probing questions? As the instructional leader of your building—this is a powerful tool.

Additionally, encourage your teachers to hold one-on-one conferences with students every week. These conferences can last five to ten minutes; it is a small sacrifice that yields impressive results—if planned correctly. Finally, quality performance assessments demonstrate how well the instructor has taught the lesson. Your teachers must be laser-focused when observing students. Well-planned lessons will allow instructors to observe the entire class simultaneously. It is during this time that important, qualitative data can be used for mandatory inventories, e.g., *Student Support Team (SST)/Response to Intervention (RTI)*. If your teachers have student-friendly, standards-aligned learning objectives, and annotated lesson plans that have been peer-reviewed, then and only then will your teachers be equipped to conduct true, meaningful observation.

The Cycle of Academic Excellence—E: Feedback

The term feedback is defined as helpful information or constructive criticism that is given to someone to inform what can be done to improve a performance, product, or service. While many people feel that any praise or evaluation falls under that umbrella, true feedback is essential information detailing how our teachers are progressing in their attempts to meet professional benchmarks. In that regard, our understanding of feedback morphs. Therefore, consider this, feedback must include three things–positive feedback and transparency, modeling measurability, and effective behavior. These three things are also known as, *The Wow, The Now,* and *The How.*

The Wow
Sometimes the positive things we see during classroom observations are obvious. Students are engaged; the teacher is prepared, enthusiastic, and genuine learning takes place. In these cases, it is easy to offer specific, positive reinforcement for what you observed. Even in situations where the lesson did not go as planned and outcomes were not where they should have been, it is essential to lead a feedback session with something positive. Be honest, but in all feedback—leave the teacher *Wow*—this burst of positivity can be the catalyst that is needed to buoy your teacher.

My daughter is a distance runner. After every race—whether it was her best, or her worst performance, I greet my baby with, *Great job! The 400 is an extremely tough race, Baby Girl!* Children are resilient, yet—they can see through a façade. Therefore, when my daughter doesn't run her race the way she practiced, it is imperative that my Wow is genuine. I find something to compliment her on—even if it's her stretching before the race. Only then is she receptive to receive constructive criticism and suggestions for improvement.

Morning Positive Walkthroughs

The Significance of the Assistant Principal

Every day, you will have interactions with several students. Your words will have an impact—positive or negative, on them for the remainder of their lives. Ensure you choose your words wisely.

--Dr. Marcus D. Jackson

The Now

It is impossible for an evaluator to give accurate feedback, or for a teacher to be receptive to change classroom outcomes, when the experience in question happened weeks ago. Timely feedback is essential, to effect sustainable change. Imagine being able to sit with a teacher and talk about a lesson that happened yesterday while it is fresh in both of your minds. Imagine being able to ask about how the students remembered the material today—to determine whether true learning had taken place. Timely feedback is the cornerstone of crucial conversations surrounding teaching and learning.

Not only does timely feedback help both parties to recall the experience accurately, but it also encourages the development of difficult, procedural skills while preventing the reinforcement of faulty approaches. Should a teacher use a faulty procedure in the classroom, or spend instructional time ineffectively, timely feedback can redirect the educator's approach—ultimately aiding him or her to become more efficient, almost immediately. New teachers, especially, will find timely feedback helpful, as they continue to develop their instructional practices. Rather than having to break bad habits later, they can stay on the right track throughout their career, hopefully—with only minor adjustments along the way.

The How
The How is where the rubber meets the road. Research about how students receive feedback in the classroom has shown that children cannot convert feedback into action without working knowledge of the concepts they are trying to master. The same can be said about teachers receiving feedback about their instruction. Therefore, it is important for administrators to model the instructional behavior that they want their teachers to display. If you want them to ask open-ended questions, model several that would have been appropriate in that setting to get them thinking about their questions to students.

Once they have a model for concept mastery, it is essential to offer measurable ways for the teacher to seek improvement. As administrators, we have become so focused on the state's standards, that we forget about the students when we try to measure outcomes. Standardized test scores are not always the best way to gauge success; however, it is the measure most often used.

Learning in a classroom is not just something that occurs among students, but among teachers and administrators as well. The process of *The Wow, The Now* and *The How* of teacher feedback moves from nebulous, to a structured, effective method of learning. In its application—transparency, positive praise, and instructional modeling with a sense of urgency, can turn regular feedback experiences into a way to improve overall instruction.

The Significance of the Assistant Principal

The *What*, the *Why*, and the *How*, are three critical words to an educator. As a principal, it is imperative that you help your teachers to understand the power of these three words.

Most educators are cognizant of the *What*. And they are consistently reminded of the importance of remembering their *Why*. However, many do not comprehend the *How*.

Just as teachers' model for their students, the principal should model the *How* to the teachers, in every facet. In my opinion, the *How* is the most important of the three.

--Dr. Marcus D. Jackson

The Cycle of Academic Excellence—F: Follow Up on the Feedback

While feedback is essential, following up on that feedback is necessary. It should be time-bound as well, usually within three to five days of the observation. Ensure that you only focus on the areas of refinement. It is imperative to be interrogative, honest, and supportive when providing insight and value.

Once the feedback has been given, it is time to follow-up by demonstrating or modeling what the student should be doing. In addition, show the instructor how to assist the students who did not meet expectations, by determining where they had difficulty. By providing consistent, timely, feedback in a positive manner, you will strengthen your teachers' motivation, while highlighting areas of improvement. This is also true of students. Teachers who provide relevant, in-the-moment student feedback, will create lasting, efficacious relationships. Teachers can give comments virtually, manually on exit tickets, or during their weekly student conferences.

Instructors should also give the student an opportunity to reflect on the feedback they have received, by encouraging them to review their own work based on the rubric and the grade they received. Students can write down what they perceive to be areas of strength and weakness. Allow students to reflect on each assignment, so that they can see their progression; this will also foster persistence and confidence.

Make it your goal and your teacher's goal to help students understand and embrace feedback. During the follow-up, always take time to say at least one positive thing about a student's work. In the initial feedback—whether it's for your teachers, or for their students—there should be two areas of performance to focus on at a maximum. Students may have additional questions after the initial feedback is given. The opportunity to ask those questions and get further clarification is important. The students should also understand that feedback should not be taken negatively. Rather, it is designed to help them consider their areas of strength, as well as their areas of opportunity. They need to learn to use the feedback as a roadmap to accomplish their goals.

Figuring out what types of follow-up feedback is critical in helping students positively progress to the next level. Instructors should integrate feedback training into the curriculum for students so they will not only be comfortable with feedback, but also so students can apply these techniques to other areas of learning, as well as their everyday lives. The process hinges on students' abilities to self-reflect and self-assess before turning in the next assignment.

Provide students guiding questions:

- What are the two areas of improvement from my last assignment?
- Am I focusing on the previous two areas of improvement on my new assignment?
- Am I having difficulty grasping the concept of the assignment?
- Do I still need clarification?
- Do I know where to access resources if I need support?

While instructors should provide feedback to their students, they should also consider implementing a student feedback component within their classrooms. By doing this, instructors will receive honest feedback from the students to determine if they are hitting the mark or missing important pieces of the puzzle. By asking the right questions, they can give students the time and encouragement to provide quality answers that will support creating and sustaining a safe, rigorous learning environment. Asking for feedback will help instructors improve their professional knowledge, as well as how they interact with their students. Look at the benefits of a robust learning environment that supports risk-taking.

Student Engagement
By soliciting student feedback, student engagement will increase. How will the instructor know what activities their students liked? How will they know what encouraged student learning if they don't ask? By learning what students liked and disliked about the assignments, as well as the teaching methods, teachers give their students a voice. Students can provide insight to lesson design aspects that will keep them engaged and immersed in learning.

Less Disciplinary Infractions
Most administrators understand that a well-planned lesson mitigates off-task behavior. When instructors understand how their students learn, they improve the dynamic of the entire class. This aids in improving classroom management, by providing an environment where the students are prepared and excited to learn.

Differentiation

Students learn differently. That's a powerful statement, because in and of itself, while the connotation may seem trite, the denotation bears weight. A great instructor will differentiate through content, process, and product—depending on their students' needs. Assessments and good grades don't tell a student's entire story. A teacher may have some students who grapple with concepts, but still persevere to achieve good grades. Conversely, there may be other students who may not feel as if they are being challenged enough, and as a result—they shun their daily tasks. If these students were only seen as their assessment data, the teacher may overlook the opportunity to challenge some of the students. There must be a balance, and this balance can only be determined through observation and feedback. The teacher should then use this feedback to differentiate the instructional delivery model to support all student learning.

The Significance of the Assistant Principal

As an assistant principal, it's imperative that you keep the triangle connected. As the assistant principal, you will have more contact with parents than anyone in the building. There is a plethora of issues that can destroy the relationship between the parent, student, and school (administration and teachers).

--Dr. Marcus D. Jackson

Essential 10:

Keep the Triangle Connected: Parents, Student, School (Administration and Teachers)

- Find a Need Fill the Gap (Be Extraordinary)

Parents can participate at school by helping with functions and activities or communicating with teachers and administrators. They can also be involved at home in many ways, including guiding their children to manage homework and other commitments and engaging in discussions about values and attitudes regarding education. It is critical that the communication between the teachers, parents, and administrators is rock solid.

Second only to the secretary the assistant principal will be in contact with more parents and stakeholders than any other person in the building. Whether it's dealing with a referral from students, being the bridge between a conflict between a teacher and parents or teacher and student, and at times the principal and teacher, a key responsibility of the assistant principal is to keep the triangle of support and collaboration connected.

As an assistant principal, it is very important to identify the purpose (the student) and two goals (outcome of the meeting) of any meeting. Next, present the triangle of support and collaboration. During the presentation it's important to:

1.) Write the child's name in the center and remind them and any others in the meeting that goal of the meeting is to keep the child at the center of all discussions.
2.) Inform the parent of the extraneous variables that are trying to infiltrate the Triangle of Support.
3.) Complete the meeting utilizing the F.U.R.R Communication Script

When it's time to have a difficult conversation with a parent, it's important to utilize the F.U.R.R. communication method:

F- **Facts** – state the facts only.
U- **Understand** the employee's situation.
R- **Respect** – always be respectful.
R- **Responsibility** – remind them of their responsibility.

Example for Meeting Difficult Parent
Greetings Mrs. Johnson. First, I would like to thank you for your visit. It's always a pleasure to meet with parents. I would like to begin the meeting by placing your son Anthony in the center of the triangle. This triangle is called "The Triangle of Success and Collaboration." This triangle signifies that the teacher, administration, and parent must form a triangle around the child, to ensure the child reaches their optimal level. As you can see there are plenty of things on the outside waiting to attack the child and it is our responsibility to keep the triangle connected. The purpose of this meeting is to: 1) hear your concerns; and 2) come to a resolution. Our goal is to do what's in the best interest of Anthony to ensure he receives a

world class education and have a productive experience at school.

Allow parent to begin voicing their concerns while you're writing. Once she has completed voicing her concerns read everything to her to be sure you didn't miss anything.

Once she's finished, begin your F.U.R.R process (This should already be scripted)

Facts - You're not pleased with your child's teacher. He says she doesn't like him; she doesn't call on him, and she's mean to him. Therefore, you would like him moved to another class. Am I correct?

Understand - I truly understand your concern. However, preparing classroom rosters is a collaborative effort amongst all staff members and administrators in the building. This process begins in the spring can take several weeks and go well into the summer. Many factors go into creating a classroom roster. The personality of the student and teacher, the involvement level of the parents, the personalities of the parents, how many students are receiving exceptional services, students who are being pulled out for small group intervention, how many boys and girls are in the class, the academic levels of the students (don't want all of the low performing students in one class), which kids had a tough time getting along with specific students the previous year, and at times, which kids socialize more when they're around specific students. Again, this process can take several weeks to complete.

Respect - I respect and appreciate your concern. However, a request such as this, not only does this affect your child and the teacher's classroom they're moving to, but it also affects the schedule of so many other students receiving services, the schedule of the support teachers providing interventions for your child and others, it affects the culture of the classroom, and may affect the teacher's schedule itself. Therefore, let's do something before considering moving your child.

Responsibility - We have a duty and responsibility to provide your child with the best education and experience at school. Therefore, Let's set up a meeting with the teacher with an open mind to voice your concern. Also, it's important to understand that in elementary school we're preparing students to be able to adapt to multiple teachers with multiple personalities. This is what they'll see in middle school. This is excellent for the social development of the child. During this meeting with the teacher, we will establish a communication plan to provide updates on your area of concern.

Most importantly, understand that we have the same goal and that is for your child to receive a world-class education, in a safe and nurturing environment, and for them to reach their full potential.

Understand - I understand you have some pers
This technique usually takes about 10 minutes, but no longer than 15 minutes. There's no additional discussion as everything was stated during the F.U.R.R process. Finally, parent, assistant principal, and teacher (if available) sign the documentation stating the meeting was held. This has been a very effective strategy for difficult conversations and an essential strategy in keeping the triangle of success and collaboration connected.

Morning Positive Walkthroughs

TRIANGLE OF SUCCESS AND COLLABORATION

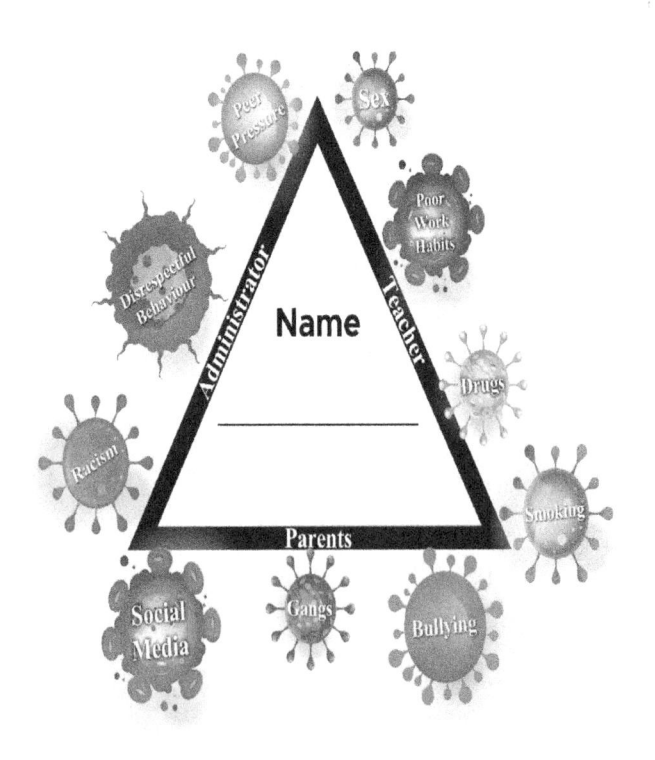

© Marcus Jackson

- **Find a Need Fill in the Gap**

Educating Teachers:140 Students Intentionally Left Behind

As an assistant principal, Dr. Jackson had an opportunity to have an amazing mentor and had some of the best teachers in the country. This was also the time he was introduced to what goes on behind the scenes in education. He never forgot the back-to-school ceremony where the staff celebrated making AYP (Annual Yearly Progress) for consecutive years. The teachers were excited, the food was great, and the staff even did the cupid shuffle. This was destined to be an awesome year. Digger deeper into the data he realized that students in 3rd, 4th, and 5th grade only needed a score of 52% to pass the test and the school only needed 59.9% of students to reach that mark. He immediately became sick. What really surprised him was that many teachers did not know about this 52%. Teachers just knew the child needed an 800 to pass and of course they knew about the 59.9%. Of course, the teachers stepped their game up another notch when they found out about the 52%.

Well midway through his first year after completing the February benchmark which would tell exactly where students were six weeks before the test. The school leadership team and district representative met and were identifying what many schools call "bubble students." The subjects discussed were looking at reading and math scores as social studies and science at the school wasn't too concerned about these content areas as they subject didn't count towards AYP.

The results from the benchmark came in and there were 140 students who weren't even close to being where they needed to be. At this point the school designed a plan of action for almost 180 students who were close to meeting the target "bubble students." Additionally, extra resources were bought in, and personnel was pulled from within the building to achieve this 59.9%. Dr. Jackson literally watched the excel file of 140 students be pushed to the side. Well, the school reached their target and did the cupid shuffle the following year during pre-planning as they meet the state requirements. That was he watched students being pushed to the side.

After the celebration, he explained what he had saw. The teachers were blown away That year, the school had a record year the following year as all subgroups were at the top of achievement in the district. Unfortunately, he and his teachers realized this was a common practice in the country (No Child Left Behind) as they were attempting to reach a very low target, but in the process, leaving so many kids behind. From that point on the school had one goal and that was for 100% of their students to excel academically.

By finding the need and filling the gap of educating teachers on the grading of standardized testing teachers were equipped with the knowledge on how it can appear that the school is doing well and still leaving many students behind. The principal eventually met with Dr. Jackson and commended him on shifting the thought process of meeting the results on the state assessment. The school went on to become one of highest performing elementary schools in the district. Therefore, it's imperative for assistant principals to find a need and fill the gap.

Bonus:
Most Essential of the Essentials:
Reflect, Revise, Write, and Relax

There were many days that I was so busy that I forgot to eat—even forgotten that I was hungry, until my stomach growled on my way home. This is an unhealthy practice, all too common to administrators, and it is a recipe for disaster. Just as I scheduled my observations, I had to schedule time for lunch. However, being so busy, I would not adhere to this schedule unless my teachers, and my office staff helped me. My office staff would usually stop me and say, Dr. J.—it's time to eat! Additionally, if teachers and students saw me in the hall, they reminded me to stop. This was powerful, because there were almost no office referrals during this time, as teachers and students knew that this was time that me and my AP were eating lunch. We only scheduled 30 minutes, but usually we only took 15-20 minutes.

As a new or veteran administrator, or school leader, you must maintain a work-life balance to avoid burnout. At the end of every day, I recommend reflecting, revising, and then relaxing.

Reflect
Each day take a few minutes to reflect; this can help you get a firm grasp on what you are doing with your time. Have you ever finished your day, saddled with more tasks to accomplish, despite not having completed your tasks on your list? It is easy for time to slip away. One way to account for one's time is to reflect on all the tasks of the day—evaluate if you did them well and decide if you needed to make some revisions.

Revise
Now that you have a good understanding of what you did or did not do, it is time to revise your methods so the next day can be even more productive. If you did not think that you accomplished your tasks in a timely manner, or if you did not complete them as well as you should have, now is the time to change your methods so you can move forward. Outline what needs to be changed. Set new deadlines and create a new schedule.

Write
As an assistant principal it is important to keep a daily journal on what you would do differently if you were the principal of the school. In this section you should write down a few things you would do differently. Some of these things you will be able to share with your principal, some of them you'll have to wait until you get your own school.

Relax
Lastly, it is important to relax as you go home, or before bed. Leave work—at work. This is the only way to continuously get the rest you need to take on the next day, fully charged. Put work aside in your mind and simply breathe and relax—even if it is only for a little while.

These steps are critical to success, and they can really help you prioritize, and stay grounded. If you complete these ten, daily essential steps—not only will you feel more accomplished, but you will also have less overall stress.

Every day after school, I meet with my AP to reflect on the day. Then we make revisions on how to make the next day better. However, before leaving, I close my door, turn the light off, turn on the lamp, play the ocean station on Pandora, close my eyes, and take about ten minutes to breathe deeply—to relax before leaving the building. Once I decompress, I leave everything at the school.

As I reflect on my thirteen years as an administrator, these are the ten things I did every single day. Although, about 100 other items can be added to this list, I found these to be important. However, the most important thing that I did not list—is that I laugh at least fifteen times per day at school. Yes, I keep count. Laughter lowers blood pressure, reduces stress hormones, and relaxes muscle tension. It's another critical component to establish and maintain a positive culture. Being a principal is one of the toughest jobs you will ever do; however, you have options. You can either run the day, or the day will run you. Ensuring these ten things are done will help you run the day.

Eat Lunch and Drink Plenty of Water

> *The Significance of the Assistant Principal*
>
> *This year will be your best year ever. I am betting on you, and I am rooting for you.*
>
> *~Dr. Marcus D. Jackson*

References

https://www.thoughtco.com/components-of-a-well-written-lesson-plan-2081871

https://www.waterford.org/resources/strategies-for-teaching-students-how-to-annotate/

https://www.facultyfocus.com/articles/teaching-and-learning/why-doesnt-teacher-feedback-improve-student-performance/

http://www.ascd.org/publications/educational-leadership/sept12/vol70/num01/Seven-Keys-to-Effective-Feedback.aspx

Made in the USA
Coppell, TX
11 May 2022